BELIEVE
TO
ACHIEVE

SYLVESTER BELL

DEDICATION

This book is dedicated to my Mother

MY MOTHER

I know this special lady who likes to praise the Lord
She does things the Bible says like making a joyful noise.
She always has a smile on her pretty face
encouraging you to walk this beautiful Christian race.

Sometimes I notice her when she comes in the door
Giving God praise, dancing on the floor.
My mother is a jewel and that's what I want to say
She always wants God to have his own way.

She is lovable, enjoyable, and very persistent too
Understanding to the things that God wants her to do.
I am so glad my mom is sweet as gold.
The way she moves and praises God
Keeps her from looking old!

Believe

to

Achieve

SYLVESTER BELL

Staleon Group
Publications
St. Louis • Orlando

Cover Photography by Nina Ingram
Cover Design by Darrell Lobin

1st Edition
ISBN: 978-0-9997880-9-7
Printed in the United States of America.

Published by:
STALEON GROUP PUBLICATIONS
P.O. BOX 592203
ORLANDO, FL 32859-2203
www.StaleonGroup.com

The Staleon Group Publication logo is a trademark of Staleon Group Publications.

Staleon Group

TABLE OF CONTENTS

ACKNOWLEDGEMENTS

Thank you to all of my friends and family that have supported me over the years. I would like to stop and just give thanks to everyone who has been there for me. I truly love each and every one of you, from the bottom of my heart.

And to my Lord and Savior… Thank You GOD!

With all my Love,

Sylvester Bell

Believe to Achieve

What would you do
To support one another?
Just show some love
And respect each other!

What would you do
If you want to please your wife?
Why not show her love
Because she's part of your life.

What would you do to
Show love toward your guy,
Express how you feel
With a wink in your eye!

What would you do to
Show love toward your girl,
Present her a gift card
Because she's part of your world!

*****

When we trust God
And do what He says,
You will be blessed
In a very special way!

That's why we depend on Him
To take us through our storm,
He will never leave us
And always extend His arm!

*****

God made the stars, moon, and sun
and placed them in the sky.
Just look at his amazing creation
God is better than good, no lie!

Man have some good doctors
and they can see your heart too
Two things they can't see
Is your spirit and soul in you!

God sent His only son
So we have the right to live.
No wonder God is better than good
Because his love is on-going for real!

God is not slack of His word
He is a man who shall never lie,
If He promise things in your life
It will happen before you die!

Please don't under estimate God
Things He's able to do,
What's too hard for man
God will give it to you!

I want you to understand
I praise him because I could,
Now I know for sure
God is better than good!

*****

We don't become successful
By starting from the top,
You must plant the seed
And water them to sprout!

*****

Stay on Guard

We must take care of our bodies
God made us using clay,
As we get older in this life
Our body parts start to decay.
We need to stay on guard
Don't know the day or hour,
Please continue to hold on
And expect his return with power!

*****

People can say some negative things
And you feel like throwing up your hands,
Let nobody side track you
The things you have planned!

*****

Never feel like you're not good enough
To reach your ultimate goal,
Continue to strive for success
And watch how it will unfold!

*****

When you woke up this morning
You received a wonderful prize,
Because of His amazing grace
He opened up your eyes! !

*****

When we on the same team
Why not support each other,
We all have challenges,
Let's try to get alone with one another!

*****

God shows us His awesome love
And extend His grace too,
That's the reason why
He will bring us through!

*****

It's a blessing to have a lady
When she can show you love,
Continue to support each other
With lots of kisses and hugs.

*****

Whatever you may need
Believe it's already done,
Hope you understand
The power is in your tongue!

Stay focus on dreams
Please don't stop,
Keep your eyes on the prize
And I promise it won't flop!

*****

Open the flood gates of Heaven
Watch the drops of rain,
That's the sign of joy
To heal your misery and pain!

*****

When you are thankful for small things
Greater blessings are ahead,
That's why you work everyday,
So you can break that bread!

*****

He deserves our worship
Don't walk around in a daze,
Continue to trust God
Because His name is so amazing and worthy to be praised!

He woke me up this morning
Clothed in my right mind,
I am so grateful
His love is so divine!

*****

When you look in the mirror
Who do you see,
God's great creation and say it's me.
No one is better than you can be
Speak to yourself and declare yourself free!

*****

You may know some people
Who always criticize,
Remember one thing,
You may need to cut the ties.
All those haters, stiff necked folks
That did you wrong
Maybe it's time for you to move on!

*****

Some people have mansions
And keep secrets not told,
What do you rather have
Than all the silver and gold?

*****

We're above and not beneath
The head and not the tail,
One thing I know for sure
His Word will prevail!

*****

Some people live for fortune
And others live for fame,
One thing I know
God love is the same!

*****

Speak to a dead situation
Watch it comes alive,
Look to the hill for help
And continue to walk and strive!

Thankful for a new day
Press toward the mark,
It gives you the opportunity
To get it right in your heart!

*****

We put our trust in a chair
When we sit down,
Why not depend on God
To turn your life around!

*****

Stay focus on your dreams,
They don't come on a silver platter.
Keep your eyes on the prize,
Your vision all that matters!

*****

Mom thank you for your love
You gave over the years,
I know some days were a struggle
But you never lived in fears!

A mother love is genuine
Morning, noon, and night.
Keep her legacy in your heart
It will help you to do what's right!

*****

God will fix your problems
In his own special way,
Just tell him thank you
On this brand new day!

*****

When you in relationship
You definitely want it to last,
Just remember one thing
Don't look back at what happened in the past!

*****

Tell yourself you can make it
Don't look at your past,
Continue to press forward
Your break-through will come at last!

You are a true friend
There through thick and thin,
I want you to know
I promise you will win!

*****

I can't let this day go by
Without given God some glory,
Today is a special day,
A reason to share the story.

*****

When God supplies your needs
He opens up his treasure,
The love he has for you
No one can measure.

*****

People want to be recognized
For everything they do,
Continue to stay faithful
And your gift makes room for you!

I remember back in the day
They had neighborhood schools,
The teachers used a paddle
To help students obey the rules.

*****

You put your life in jeopardy
When you disobey God's will.
Stay on the look-out,
Because the Devil is for real.

*****

It's good to support your wife
In everything she does,
You never have to wonder
Why she shows you love!

*****

It's an honor to be a father
I believe you're doing your part,
Keep the love of son/daughter
And I promise they won't part!

Some people act like big shots
And live above their means,
Don't get side tracked
Stay focus on your dreams!

*****

Strive to reach your goals
Stand to complete your test
Keep your eyes on the prize
And maintain the thrill and zest!

*****

When everything is said and done
Rise above your storm,
God is in control
To protect you from all harm!

*****

Now don't get it twisted
When the devil comes again,
Remember one thing
In God you will win!

You are an awesome woman
Your words are rich and wise,
When temptations come
Protect your gift with pride.

*****

Your success is the goal
And you will achieve,
You have to encourage yourself
And continue to believe!

*****

You are an awesome man
And you have integrity too,
No one can stop your plan
Your business you decided to do!

*****

Just Listen

Sometimes we have to count to five
Because our behavior is out of control,
We must remain calm
And the situation will unfold!

*****

Stay Calm.

We're not gonna make any progress
Yelling, screaming with our voice.
The best solution we can do is to listen,
That is the best choice!

*****

Please continue to move forward

If you want to make gains,
Let nothing weigh you down
Because your purpose is to maintain!

*****

We don't become successful
On a silver platter,
The things you're going through
It really does matter.
When you walk in doors,
You have style and fashion
Now I understand why
You have love and passion.

*****

I can't tell you enough
How I appreciate your love
Continue to be humble
because you so beautiful as a dove!

*****

About the Author

ABOUT THE AUTHOR

Sylvester Bell was born November 3, 1958 in St. Louis, Missouri. He has been married to Camille Bell for over 30 years, and has one son, Sylvester Bell, Jr.

Sylvester graduated from Vashon High School in 1977. Bell then went on to further his education at Harris Stowe State College. Sylvester graduated from Harris Stowe in 1982 and transitioned into his teaching career.

Sly, as most people affectionately call him, began working for the St. Louis Public School system in 1983. Sylvester taught at Hamilton Branch Elementary then at Buder Elementary School, where he taught 4th and 5th grade for 26 years. Bell completed the final three years of his career at Shenandoah Elementary School. After 30 years of dedicated service, Sylvester Bell retired from the St. Louis Public School System in 2013.

Today, Sylvester Bell serves as an Assistant Pastor at the National Memorial St. Louis Holy Temple Church of God in Christ. He is also proudly employed as a host at the famous Goody Goody Diner in St. Louis, where he shares his love and passion to assist and encourage guests with his poetic talent and skills!